I Wonder...

Author & Photographer – Donnah M. Cole

A Read Along Children's Book
- Faith in God -

In Memory of my Dad,
who no longer needs faith,
because now he knows!

White clouds move
across the vast blue sky.

I wonder who hung them
up so high.

A quiet wind whispers through the great oak trees.

I wonder why I can't see the gentle breeze.

The swans and ducks
drift past the shore.

I wonder what inspires them
to always explore.

Drops of water
over the edge do flow.

I wonder where the
droplets travel and go.

The bright moon glows in the deep dark night.

I wonder what makes it shine so bright.

The garden flowers
do not labor or spin.

I wonder who painted
their beauty within.

The golden fields of grain
seem to wave at me.

I wonder what secrets hide
within their seeds.

The bay whispers,
"Come walk upon the ocean blue."

I wonder who would hold me, so I
wouldn't fall through.

Mountains, majestic, inspire my soul.

I wonder what mysteries they eternally hold.

Silence and stillness are
gifts of the snow.

I wonder what makes
the flakes icy cold.

The sun rises and sets,
sparking fire in the sky.

I wonder how it chases away
the shadows of the night.

Seagulls soar over the ocean so blue.

I wonder if they enjoy the magnificent view.

I marvel at these mysteries of old and wonder who created their beauty to behold.

**Created by Someone I cannot see,
who spoke…
and something (out of nothing) came to be.**

A universe, spectacular,
proclaims His Deity.

I put my faith in the One
who wonderfully created me.

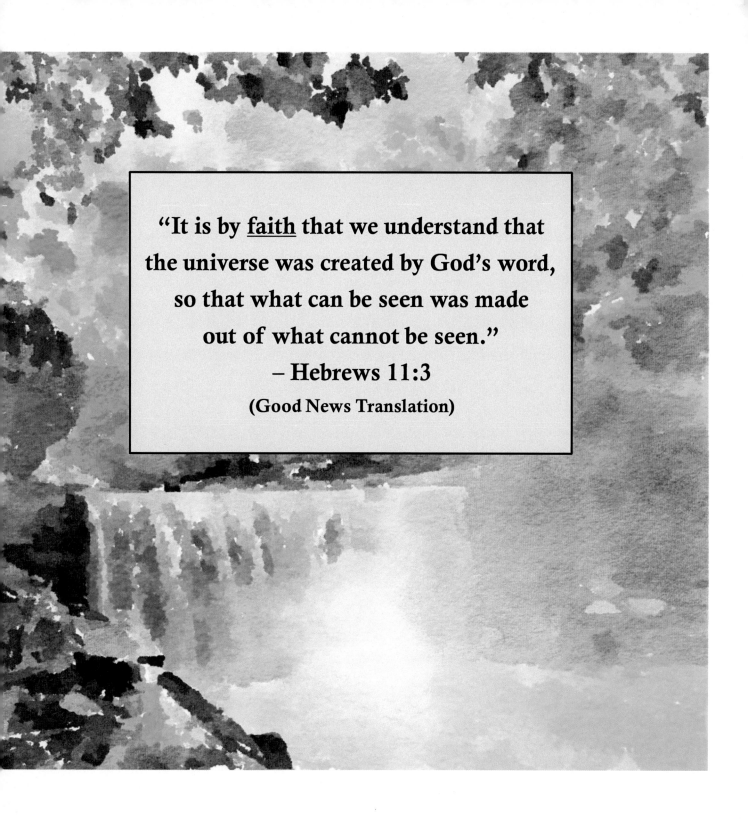

"It is by <u>faith</u> that we understand that the universe was created by God's word, so that what can be seen was made out of what cannot be seen."
– Hebrews 11:3
(Good News Translation)

Photography Locations:

Cover & Copyright – Old Fort, NC

Dedication – Old Fort, NC

1 – Ixonia, WI

2 – Candler, NC

3 – Creeper Trail, Damascus, VA

4 – Lake Junaluska, NC

5 – Multnomah Falls, OR

6 – Hyatt Creek, Waynesville, NC

7 – Haywood Comm College, Clyde, NC

8 – Old Fort, NC

9 – Charleston, SC

10 – Blue Ridge Parkway, NC

11 – Old Fort, NC

12 – Waterrock Knob, Blue Ridge Parkway, NC

13 – Folly Beach, SC

14 – Turnpike Ridge, Candler, NC

15 – Angel Oak Tree, Johns Island, SC

16 – Pretty Place, NC/SC Border

17 – Cumberland Falls, KY

18 – Erwin, TN

Dear precious one,

Please know
you are
deeply loved
by the Lord God
who does wonders!

(Psalm 77:14)

Available on Amazon:

Travel with Papa Pepper, Mother Fern, and their six ducklings as they journey to their new home. Laugh with them, hope for them, and cheer them on, as they paddle through the great unknown!

Made in the USA
Las Vegas, NV
29 September 2021